the sweetest kind of poison

katie wismer

D1464965

the sweetest kind of poison copyright © 2018 Katie Wismer. All rights reserved. Printed in the United States of America. This book or any portion thereof may not be reproduced or used in any manner whatsoever without the express written permission of the publisher except for the use of brief quotations in a book review.

cover design: Christina Hitchmough

https://sdwismer.wixsite.com/katiewismer

First Edition
ISBN-13: 978-1720864523
ISBN-10: 1720864527

to the people who held me up
when I couldn't stand on my own

to you

my hands were covered
in the ink
he made my heart bleed
so I dried them
on these pages

and so these words are for you
dear reader

because I need you to know

that you are not a victim
you are not broken
and you will be just fine
without
him

contents

i.
the fall

I'm going to tell you a story
don't worry
it has a happy ending
but maybe not the kind you're used to

because in this story
the guy doesn't get the girl
the princess doesn't find her knight
there isn't a beautiful wedding
or a happily ever after

in this story
that knight in shining armor?
the one with messy brown hair
and an earth-shattering smile?

well
he turns out to be the bad guy

the stories never tell you what to do
when the knight who rescues you
turns out to be more dangerous
than the dragon he saved you from

but even without a rulebook
and no guidelines to follow
I think I figured it out

here's how I survived

it's probably hard to understand
if you've never been a little girl
with a notebook, a fluffy blue pen
and dreams of princes and love stories
lulling you to sleep

it's probably hard to understand
if you've never been in high school
and watched every pretty girl
get invited to the dance
and left wondering why
nobody asked you

it's probably hard to understand
if you've never fallen for a boy
who you thought was too good for you
and been completely blinded by surprise
when he wanted you back

it's probably hard to understand
even if you have done these things
because I'm still trying to understand it myself

my young heart saw your
dark eyes and jagged edges
and thought
oh
what a fun adventure it would be
to be broken by you

he was that first alcoholic drink
you sneak when you're fifteen years old
and you feel like you're
getting away with something

he was that fleeting moment
when your flight hits some turbulence
and you think just maybe
this could be it

he was that acoustic guitar
on the nights you couldn't sleep
that followed you
into your dreams

he was everything I didn't need
disguised as everything I wanted

my heart was made of fire
and you were gasoline

    we burned
        and burned
            and burned
                and burned

but never once were we
touched by the flames

it seemed like some kind of
m a g i c

she was just a girl
with a hard shell
a soft heart
and some heavy dreams
in her pockets

he was just a boy
with a sharp tongue
some wandering eyes
and too few cares
in the world

I wanted you
because I liked the idea
of you wanting me

my heart begged me
not to be so reckless
but you were too much of a thrill
to resist

you were just my type
and darling
your lips
were so deceiving

how was I to stand a chance?

I guess sometimes
you find someone perfect for you
in every way
except for the ways that matter

I'm just trying to understand
how being with you
can feel like heaven and hell
all at once

I will never understand it
I don't have enough time
I don't have enough ink

all this time
I thought I could swim

because there are oceans inside of me
and I've spent my whole life
learning to tread water

but then you came along
and it was everything I could do
to stop myself
from drowning

you might be fun
and passion
and danger
and risk
but my soul is hungry
for so much more
than just your hands
on my skin

you made me feel the fire
but all I wanted
was to be sheltered from the storm

I fell for a version of you
that doesn't exist

I am no longer holding out
for you to see the light
I think it's time
that I do

ii.
the collapse

it was a car crash
in the dead of night

twisted metal
headlights smeared across my vision
an all-consuming pain

I didn't even realize anything was wrong
until the entire world
was upside down

-*blindsided*

how silly of me
to think I was special
when to you
I was just one of many

how silly of me
to ignore the warnings
of the girls you discarded
before you met me

and how silly of me
to give myself to you
when I should have known
you couldn't do the same

sometimes you think you found a good one
but then he turns out to be just another
monster wearing a mask

you did everything you could
to get me to trust you enough
to let you crack open my chest
so you could look inside
but I guess you didn't like what you found

at least not enough

it's an art
really
the way you twist your cruelest words
into a nice little bow
and somehow convince me
that I tied the knot

your words used to make me melt
now all they do is burn

did you say the same things to her that night?
if you were to replace my name
with some other girl's
would anything
be different
at all?

your lies were like drops of acid
once I was touched by one
it just spread
and festered
and burned its way through
everything you had ever done

if he leaves you with silence for 2 weeks
and then comes crawling back
it isn't because he misses you
it's because he couldn't find anyone else

and so I stopped
picking up when you called
because I realized
all the rumors had been true
and all of your promises
were paper-thin

and so I stopped responding

that is
until I didn't

you may not be the sun
but still
I looked at you for so long
and now that I've looked away
my eyes cannot adjust
and everything just looks
dark

it's easy to say
I don't need you
when you're still here
but it's so hard to remember
after you leave

I deserve better
but I prefer you

I wish I could want what's good for me
as badly as I want you

- can you be addicted to a person?

what is it called
when you stay with someone
who does nothing
but hurt
manipulate
and lie
to you?

~~weakness~~
abuse.

your love just feels like a punishment

I don't care
if I was the one
you always came back to
it should have been me
every time

your kind words
mean nothing
if you have to be drunk
to say them

why would I want your mouth on me
now that I know all the places it's been?

-you're just another bad habit to kick

sometimes you think you've found the one
and you're wrong

and it's not losing him that hurts
it's losing that hope

it's the exhaustion that follows
as you think about all the time it takes
to get to know a person

to build that foundation
to talk to him
in a way you don't talk to anyone else

and wondering what was the point
of all that time
of all those conversations
of all those late nights
if he was just going to leave

and realizing you'll have to start all over
with someone else

- *I'm just so fucking tired of dead ends*

I can't love you into being a good person

49

I fell in love with your shadow
a cursory glimpse at most
and even though you claim to still be here
all I feel is your ghost

iii.
the withdrawal

you don't deserve a book
a poem
or even a word
but yet here I am
wasting all of my ink on you

I wish I could light a match inside of my skull
and burn your name from my memory
like the scraps of paper
filled with the words
you've made my heart scream

she missed him
she missed talking until 3 in the morning
and the way everything got lighter when he called
she missed the way he said her name
and the danger that came with every move he made
but she didn't miss the random weeks of silence
or the doubts and insecurities
she didn't miss wondering which girl he hit on
tonight
while she wasn't around
or whether or not he was sleeping alone
she missed him
but she didn't

loving you
leaving you—
it all hurts
just the same

he's not worth
the six times
you check your phone
waiting for a response

he's not worth
the burning in your eyes
that you pretend isn't there
when he says something mean

he's not worth
the extra hours you stay awake
just to talk to him
when he can't sleep

he's not worth
destroying yourself over
trust me

the sound of your name
still gives me bruises

I'm just trying to remember
what I wanted
before you

every time you miss him so much
that you start to convince yourself
maybe the abuse wasn't so bad
I want you to remember this:

he doesn't care
if you're okay

he doesn't care
if you're unhappy

he doesn't care
if he hurts you

he doesn't care
about you
at all

so many things have been ruined for me
because they make me think of you

sometimes happiness feels so fragile

I guess that's the problem
with small towns
everywhere I look
is stained with memories
of you
there's no place
you haven't touched

somehow the healing
hurts worse than the breaking

and now all of my nightmares
are dressed like you

the worst feeling
is being drunk
at 3 am

after everyone else
has gone home

and you find yourself
alone
with the room spinning

and despite all the shots
and the wine
and the beer
and the lights
and the people

at the end of the night
it's just you

climbing into bed
bracing your hand against the wall

and you realize
goddamn
I still miss him

no matter where I go
or who I meet
or what I see
I only want
to talk
to you

my days are too empty without you
there's so much space
you used to fill

you and I
were never art by any means
but damn
the days have so much less color
now that you're gone

- *I'm not ready to be strangers again*

I can't decide if you don't care
or if you're sitting there
convincing yourself
that if I cared
I'd reach out
just like I'm telling myself
about you

3 letters
8 minutes
that's all it took
for me to fall back into your web

-hey

I mistook a relapse
for a second chance

-some things end for a reason

because of you
I have the urge to break things
I want to see glass shatter
into a million pieces
and feel ribs crack
beneath my hands

because of you
I have the urge to scream
I want to scream as loudly as I can
until my throat tears open
and fills with blood

because of you
I have the urge to drown
I want to cry until my tears
fill the room around me
and swallow me whole

but even then
I don't think it would be enough
even then
I wouldn't have any peace
even then
your ghost wouldn't leave me

it's too easy to forget
you're a battleground
when you feel so much
like coming home

I keep blaming you
for reopening my wounds
but I'm the one
who keeps letting you

you must have some kind of gravity
we must have some kind of magnetic pull
there must be a reason
it feels so unnatural
to let you go

maybe I'm just a little too good
at accepting things
that are just "good enough"

I just want someone to want me
even after they see the shadows
even if we're not naked
even if sometimes
I don't know how to want myself

it doesn't take much
to want you
but it takes a lot
to want myself again
after you leave

I think it's really beautiful
the way you smile around your tears
and laugh even when it hurts
like knives in your stomach

I think it's really brave
the way you climbed back to your feet
after he tried to break you

but you just dusted off your shoulders
and walked away
even though a part of you
wanted to stay

you are not giving up by leaving
you are choosing to love yourself
more than he ever could

I'm so glad I was never the girl
you wanted me to be
I don't think I would have liked her much

he was the sweetest kind of poison
but poison nonetheless

if you must break
then break
if you must cry
then cry
but don't let him make you bitter
he may have stolen your heart
but don't let him steal your light

no one who's meant for you
would let you go so easily

he's gone
and that hurts
but not as much as it hurt
when he was here

iv.
the recovery

I wish I could take time
like a pill
to heal these wounds

how to survive the heartbreak:

i. read poetry from those who have been there before
ii. watch movies you loved before you met him
iii. listen to songs that make you want to dance
iv. run. I know it fucking sucks but put on some angry music and *run*
v. eat lots of fruit
vi. put on your favorite outfit and leave the house
vii. get as much fresh air as you can
viii. spend time with your friends, even if you think you don't want to
ix. delete his number so you can't call
x. delete old messages so you can't reread them
xi. delete old pictures so you can't look at them
xii. don't try to find a new guy. being with yourself is enough.
xiii. let yourself break down. you don't have to be okay.
xiv. at some point stop crying
xv. it will get better. just take it one day at a time.

it took me a long time to realize
by thinking of you as
everything
I was allowing myself to be
nothing

how silly of me
to let a boy
of flesh and bone and meager intelligence
poison my mind and paralyze my heart
how silly of me
to forget
I am the stars and sun and moon
trapped inside a body
it was a blessing to lose that boy
not a tragedy

I don't need you to want me
it would be nice, yes
but I don't need it
my fire won't be any less bright
just because you are no longer
sharing its warmth

I let you be my gravity for too long

I have fallen in love
with your absence

you've made some mistakes
but today is a new day
so breathe in
breathe out
and be better

always remember
life exists outside of this moment
this isn't how it will always be
you won't always be sad
it won't always be hard
I promise you
you're going to be okay

it wasn't a waste
loving you
it taught me
everything I don't want
and everything I deserve

this pain and darkness you've caused
is the water poured on the seeds
of my poetry

I was happier with you
but I was a fool

some mornings
I sit outside
with my cup of coffee
when the sunlight is gentle
and the birds' songs are soft
and I don't even think
about you
at all

there's a sunrise every single morning
but everyone acts like
it's so rare to see one

that's just because
not everyone
is willing to put in the effort
to get up and appreciate it

you are the most stunning
of sunrises

- *find yourself an early riser*

I always thought you were the spark
but darling
the world is made of fire
and I am gasoline

the time for feeling sorry for yourself
has passed
do whatever it takes
to make yourself happy

one day he came back

but
she
wouldn't
have
him

I know you think you want me
but that girl you liked
the one who ripped everything she was
out of her chest to make room
for everything you wanted to fill inside
is no longer here
and she's never coming back

I am not a cure for your boredom

you're back
because you realized my value
but unfortunately for you
so have I

I hope every boy like you
runs into a girl like me
so she can write words like these
and you'll stop getting away with it

if you ever feel like
losing him
is the end of your world

go out and see
some part of the world
you've never seen

go meet someone
nothing like yourself

go find a culture so rich
you can taste it in the air

and I promise
you will change your mind

I'm at peace with my mistakes
at least I had good intentions with you
funny
I doubt you can say the same

111

I know you think you've won
that you broke me
but darling
my dreams
were always so much grander
than just you and I

almost romances
almost relationships
almost loves
are almost worth your time
almost
but not quite

I'm a better person without you

each day
I think of you
less and less
and that
is the greatest
mercy

can't you see?
he was never the hero of your story
it has always been you

he's a crutch
you no longer need
you can walk
you are healed
let him go

you found your revenge
through the bodies
of other girls

I found my closure
through the words
on this page

so go ahead,
have your vengeance

I'd rather have my peace

v.

the now

all I can do
is write my truths
and hope that
someone else understands

here's what no one tells you
about hitting rock bottom:
it's not a spiritual awakening
or shedding of skin
or moment of clarity

it's ugly, heaving breaths
bloody, numb fingers
tired, swollen eyes

it's not a movie montage of change
or an empowering battle cry

it's silence

it's sitting in the dark
alone
the hum of a fan
beating against the inside of your skull

it's staring your thoughts in the face
with a voiceless throat
and raw eyes
and realizing

this is me

this hopeless, sloppy, pitiful mess is me

and I am so fucking lucky to have her

122

here's what no one tells you
about the weak days:
that after you realized your worth
and peeled yourself off the floor
and made yourself walk away

that even after you met someone else
and he's just so kind
and everything is going so well

that still

there are some nights
when a few tears will escape your eyes
and you will remember a time
when his words were the last thing you heard
before falling asleep

and your fingers will itch to pick up the phone
and some days you even just might

no one likes to talk about the weak days
but in those moments
they always manage to eclipse
everything else

but here's what no one tells you about
falling in love:
sometimes it's fast, violent
the type of drop that gives you whiplash

123

and sometimes it's not

sometimes it's slow, soft
the barest whisper of a tide
inching for your toes

it's never consistent
never predictable
and the only thing that's certain
is it will happen again

I'm weird, okay?
I wear black dresses
and dance around my room
and write poetry that doesn't rhyme
and if that's not okay with you
then I'd rather be
alone

125

sometimes you just have to let yourself collapse
and rebuild

he wasn't the man
you needed him to be

he couldn't be

and it's no failure of yours
it's not even his failure

you're just two planets
who tried to make it work

but your orbits will always be
just out of sync

- I forgive you

all I know is
I'm not the same person
I was yesterday
and maybe
that's not such a bad thing

sometimes all you can do
is embrace the here

I am so sorry
to every girl I ever blamed
to every girl I ever hated
when it was always
just
him

I like poetry because
it's the only time
people ever say anything
honest

no matter what anyone
tries to tell you

make
your
art

you have no idea
how badly the world needs it

if you're scared of
someone else reading it
you're probably
doing something right

I'm chasing the day
I can write happy poems
just as easily
as the sad ones

I used to feel so empty
after you left
like there were holes
in my chest
but now my life is so full
of dreams and goals and joy
honestly
I don't think
there would even be room for you
anymore

if I could go back
and give advice to my 16-year-old self
I'd tell her to wear a little less eyeliner
a little more lipstick
and tell that boy
to go fuck himself

it's not about finding someone
to heal your broken heart
it's about finding someone
worth the risk of it breaking all over again

I want you
mess and all

I don't mind waiting
while you get back on your feet

and I'll help you
pick up the pieces
as best I can

and if there's nothing I can do
I'll sit with you
while you pick them up yourself

so at least
you don't have to do it alone

- *someone new*

I am thankful for
coffee
coffee shop music
and the poetry I write in the corner
as I think of you

your poems
your body
your dreams
your goals
do not need to look
like anyone else's

you are enough as you are

you are allowed
to take up space

stop comparing yourself
to the filtered photographs
proudly splashed across social media
of course no one posts a picture
of them crying alone
on the bathroom floor
at 2 in the morning
but that doesn't mean
you're the only one
who's done it

like me or don't
that's your choice
the important thing is
I like me
and that
darling
you get no say in

I'm just trying to be
a little kinder
than I was yesterday

I may not know who I am yet
but I sure as hell won't let you tell me

I've been writing all these words
trying to sound smart, profound

important enough to print
in one of those books
schools make you read

trying to unearth some truth
no one else has found

but then I thought

the people reading these words
the ones I write them for

well, maybe they're just like me
maybe they're just like you

and maybe you don't need
profound
smart
or iconic

maybe you just need real
honest
or familiar

so maybe I'll never say something brilliant
maybe I'll never really say anything at all

except that I'm here
and I'm just like you

searching for meaning
and myself
in whatever words I can find

so I guess that means
neither of us is alone

at the time it felt insurmountable
an albatross made of steel
pinned to my chest

but one day
the tears grew fewer
the pain felt dimmer
and suddenly
I stopped blaming myself
for everything I couldn't change

it is not okay
the way he treated you
it is not okay
the pain you felt

but you learned what you could
and you've grown as much as you can

and honestly
there's no revenge
quite like
getting up
moving on
and
doing *just fine*

connect with katie wismer

www.goodreads.com/KatesBookDate
youtube.com/c/katesbookdate
instagram: @katesbookdate & @katiewismer
twitter: @katesbookdate
sdwismer.wixsite.com/katiewismer

ABOUT THE AUTHOR

Katie Wismer is a diehard pig-lover, semi-obsessive gym rat, and longtime sucker for a well-written book. She studied Creative Writing and Sociology at Roanoke College, which you've probably never heard of, but she argues is the best school in existence.

She spends most of her free time on her YouTube channel Katesbookdate where she chats about books, life, and veganism.

Books have always been her passion projects, but *The Sweetest Kind of Poison* is the first to escape into the world.

83461564R00086

Made in the USA
Middletown, DE
11 August 2018